This book is due for return on or before the last date shown below.

1   MAR 2018

HEATWAVE

Heinemann
LIBRARY

Catherine Chambers

www.heinemann.co.uk/library

Visit our website to find out more information about **Heinemann Library** books.

To order:

 Phone ++44 (0)1865 888066

 Send a fax to ++44 (0)1865 314091

 Visit the Heinemann Bookshop at www.heinemann.co.uk/library to browse our catalogue and order online.

First published in Great Britain by Heinemann Library, Halley Court, Jordan Hill, Oxford OX2 8EJ, a division of Reed Educational and Professional Publishing Ltd. Heinemann is a registered trademark of Reed Educational & Professional Publishing Ltd.

OXFORD MELBOURNE AUCKLAND JOHANNESBURG BLANTYRE
GABORONE IBADAN PORTSMOUTH NH (USA) CHICAGO

Designed by Visual Image
Illustration by Paul Bale
Originated by Ambassador Litho Ltd.
Printed and bound in South China.

ISBN 0 431 15066 4

06 05 04 03 02
10 9 8 7 6 5 4 3 2 1

British Library Cataloguing in Publication Data

Chambers, Catherine
Heatwave. – (Wild Weather)
1. Heat waves – (Meteorology) – Juvenile literature
I. Title
551.5'253
ISBN 0431150664

Acknowledgements

The Publishers would like to thank the following for permission to reproduce photographs: Associated Press pp5, 13, 17, 19, 21, 27, Corbis pp8, 11, 15, 23, 28, FLPA p22, PA Photos (EPA) p18, Photodisc pp4, 7, 16, 20, 25, 26, Robert Harding Picture Library p9, Science Photo Library pp10, 14, Stone (Getty) pp24, 29, Tudor Photography p12.

Cover photograph reproduced with permission of Corbis.

The Publishers would like to thank the Met Office for their assistance with the preparation of this book.

Every effort has been made to contact copyright holders of any material reproduced in this book. Any omissions will be rectified in subsequent printings if notice is given to the Publisher.

Any words appearing in the text in bold, **like this**, are explained in the Glossary.

Contents

What is a heatwave?

A heatwave is a long period of very hot weather. There are no clouds to shade us from the Sun's rays and no wind to cool us down.

The heat dries up the ground. Plants **wilt** and
die. People and animals get too hot and thirsty.
They find it difficult to breathe.

Where do heatwaves happen?

Heatwaves can happen almost anywhere. Many happen in the middle of large areas of land called **continents**. These places can be far away from the cool sea.

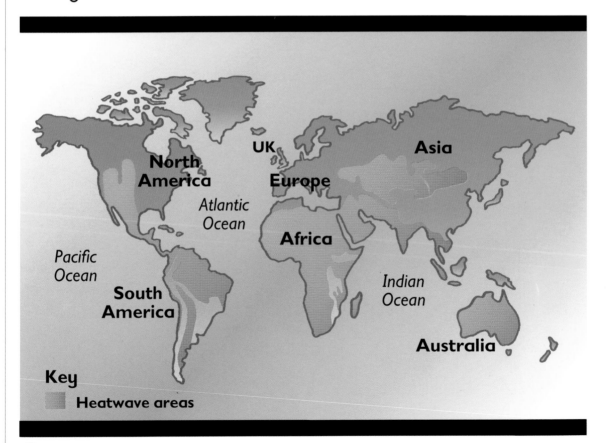

North America

UK

Europe

Asia

Atlantic Ocean

Africa

Pacific Ocean

South America

Indian Ocean

Australia

Key

Heatwave areas

Islands can suffer from heatwaves, too. The sea
is usually very calm and still when there is a
heatwave. There are no winds to cool the land.

Why is it so hot?

The weather is usually hotter in the summer. More of the Sun's heat reaches the part of the Earth we live on. Clouds can stop some of this heat from reaching us.

In this picture the sky is clear. There are no clouds to stop the Sun beating down. There is no breeze to cool the land.

Why do heatwaves happen?

Heatwaves happen when **masses** of hot air stay over one place for a long time. These are called high pressure masses. This weather map shows areas of low and high pressure.

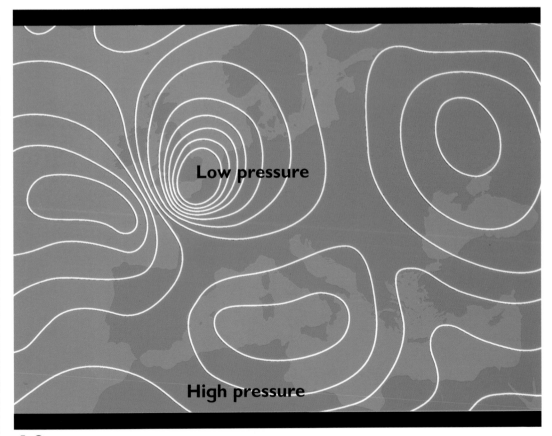

Low pressure

High pressure

Winds blow from high pressure to low pressure.
The mass of high pressure stops winds from
blowing in from other places. The air is very still.

What are heatwaves like?

During a heatwave, the **temperature** becomes very hot. This **thermometer** shows a temperature of 44°C. People cannot stay outside in this heat.

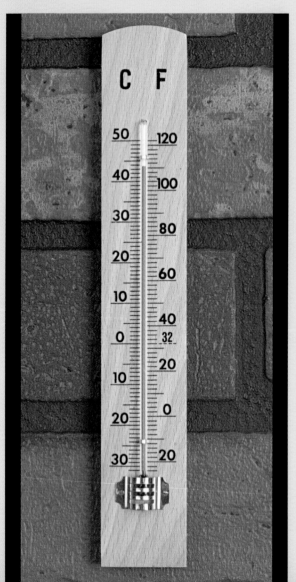

City streets are hot and dusty. The air is still and **hazy** with smelly **fumes**. Pavements get too hot to walk on.

Harmful heatwaves

There is very little wind in a heatwave. So **gases** from car engines and factory chimneys do not blow away. Cities get very **polluted**. Some people find it hard to breathe.

Things that are made of metal, like cars, become too hot to touch. When the weather is very hot, the surface of roads can melt because of the heat.

Heatwave in the city

This is Chicago in the USA. The city is in the middle of a **continent** and near a lake. So it is very hot and **humid** in the summer. When there is a heatwave it gets even hotter.

Chicago suffered a terrible heatwave in 1995.
Many people had heatstroke. This is when the
body cannot cool itself down. Some people
became very ill.

Preparing for heatwaves

Weather forecasters can find out when a heatwave will happen. They look at pictures taken by **satellites** far above the Earth. The pictures tell them what the weather will be like.

When a heatwave is coming, people buy a lot of soft drinks or bottled water. It is important to drink enough water when the weather is very hot.

Keeping cool

People put on lightweight clothes in a heatwave. Office workers often wear shorts and open-necked shirts instead of suits. Hats protect people from the burning Sun.

The best way of keeping cool is to get wet!
People walk through water sprays in parks.
Patients with heatstroke are covered in
cold water.

Coping with a heatwave

There was a long heatwave in Greece recently. The cities became hot and stuffy with **fumes** from cars and factories. People stopped driving their cars to avoid making more fumes.

People tried to shade themselves from the rays of the Sun. The hot Sun can burn your skin. You should always protect your skin from the Sun's rays by wearing suntan cream and a hat.

Animals and plants in a heatwave

When the weather is cold, this cat's fur keeps it warm. In really hot weather, cats lose some of their fur to keep cool. This is called moulting. Pets need plenty of drinking water in a heatwave.

In a heatwave plants lose the water they need more quickly. Farmers use sprinklers to make sure their **crops** have enough water.

To the rescue!

People can get heatstroke in a heatwave. They feel dizzy and sick. Sometimes they **collapse**. Ambulance workers help people to recover, or they take the patients to hospital.

Heatwaves can harm farm animals. So the
animals are herded into the shade. Farm
workers bring plenty of drinking water
in tankers.

Adapting to heatwaves

Ceiling fans or air conditioning cool down homes, offices and schools in a heatwave. At home, people also buy **rotating** fans that plug into the wall.

In some countries, buildings are designed to keep out the heat. The walls are very thick. They are painted white to reflect the Sun. The windows are small and have shutters.

Fact file

◆ Heatwaves can be so hot that **tarmac** roads melt. Metal bends and cement cracks and crumbles. Sometimes buildings and bridges become dangerous.

◆ The Chicago heatwave in 1995 lasted from July to August. It killed nearly six hundred people. Many other parts of the United States were hit by the heatwave, too.

◆ Heatwaves have caused more people to die in Australia than any other **natural disaster**.

Glossary

collapse fall

continents huge areas of land. Europe is a continent, so is Africa.

crops plants grown for food

fumes smelly harmful gases

gases light, usually invisible substance. Air contains many different gases.

hazy fuzzy and unclear

humid when air contains a lot of moisture

masses large areas or amounts of something

natural disaster disaster caused by nature, not humans

polluted spoiled with harmful gases or other substances

rotating going round and round

satellite spacecraft moving around the Earth

tarmac road surface made of little stones and sticky black tar

temperature measure of how hot or cold it is

thermometer something used for measuring temperature

weather forecasters scientists who work out what weather we will get

wilt when a plant loses

Index

32